W9-ASR-811

I KNOW AMERICA

Our
Folk
Heroes

Karen Spies

THE MILLBROOK PRESS
Brookfield, Connecticut

Published by The Millbrook Press
2 Old New Milford Road
Brookfield, CT 06804
© 1994 Blackbirch Graphics, Inc.

All rights reserved. No part of this book may be reproduced in any form
without the permission in writing from the publisher except by a reviewer.
Printed in the United States of America.

5 4 3 2 1

Created and produced in association with Blackbirch Graphics.
Series Editor: Tanya Lee Stone

Library of Congress Cataloging-in-Publication Data
Spies, Karen Bornemann.
    Our folk heroes / by Karen Spies.
    p.   cm.   — (I know America)
    Includes bibliographical references and index.
    Summary: Introduces our country's best-known folk heroes; discusses how folk
heroes develop and why we tell and retell tall tales.
    ISBN 1-56294-440-1 (lib. bdg.)
    1. Heroes—United States—Biography—Juvenile literature. 2. Legends—United
States. 3. Folklore—United States—Juvenile literature. 4. Heroes in literature—
Juvenile literature. I. Title. II. Series.
E176.S833   1994
398.2'0973—dc20   93-35013
                                                                CIP
                                                                AC

Acknowledgments and Photo Credits
Cover, p. 35: ©Blackbirch Press; pp. 5, 7, 21, 30, 34, 39, 45: The Bettmann Archive;
pp. 8, 18, 22, 25, 33, 36: The Library of Congress; pp. 11, 14, 15, 24, 27, 28, 38, 40,
42: Northwind Picture Archives; p. 44: ©Adelheid Howe, 1983.

CONTENTS

Imagine a time when there was no television to watch, no shopping malls to visit, and no movies to go to. What could people do for entertainment on long winter nights or hot summer evenings? Tell stories, of course. That's how tales of folk heroes began.

Folk heroes can be real people or made-up characters. But even when folk heroes are real, sometimes not all the details given about them are true. While these details may be based on what a person did, they are often exaggerated. For example, a soldier who killed two men in battle may be described as having defeated an entire army all by himself. Or, a person of average appearance and ability may be described as a giant with superhuman strength.

Why did storytellers change the facts? There are a number of reasons. They wanted to make their tales interesting and exciting. They admired their heroes so much that they wanted them to sound more important than anybody else. They also probably started believing that these men and women had done a lot more than they actually had. And, as the stories were told and retold over the years, the details often became confused.

Davy Crockett was a famous frontiersman from Tennessee.

Almost every region of the country has its own folk heroes. Easterners told about Ethan Allen, who fought in the Revolutionary War. From the North came tales of Paul Bunyan and Babe, his big blue ox. In the South, slaves told of the wise slave High John the Conqueror. Westerners swapped stories about the outlaw Jesse James.

The many occupations, or jobs, that were part of building this country also created folk heroes. These heroes were usually bigger, stronger, and smarter than everyone else. Sailors told about Old Stormalong and his giant ship, the *Courser*. Cowboys described how Pecos Bill supposedly tamed a cyclone and created the Grand Canyon. John Henry became the hero of railroad workers everywhere when he out-drilled a steam drill.

There is a magic in all of these tales. Folk heroes do what ordinary people can only dream of doing. They seem to live very colorful lives. Naturally, Paul Bunyan could not have scooped out the Great Lakes any more than Pecos Bill could have made the Grand Canyon. And although Jesse James was a murderer, the folk song about him makes him seem like someone to admire.

It's fun to tell folk tales, to share in the laughter and enjoy the often wild claims. There's a feeling that ties the storyteller to every other storyteller who has told the tale. There's the excitement of asking, "Have you heard this?" Trying to outdo other storytellers is a big part of the tradition of folk tales.

Folk heroes are as much a part of American history as are important historical events. Molly Pitcher showed great courage as a heroine in the Revolutionary War. With the lure of the frontier came the tales of Davy Crockett. Hiawatha is known for his great efforts to make peace between Native Americans during the mid-1500s. The rowdy life of the Wild West is captured in the tales of Calamity Jane and Nat Love, a cowboy who became known as Deadwood Dick.

Is there a place for folk heroes today? Television and movies have certainly drawn attention away from storytelling. On the other hand, certain folk heroes, like Davy Crockett and Mike Fink, have become more well known because of television. Times have really changed, and we no longer have the same types of heroes. But we still enjoy reading about the men and women who fought in our country's early battles, tamed the wilderness, and worked on riverboats and plantations.

This book includes stories about some of these rugged individuals. It also explores stories about folk heroes such as Johnny Appleseed, who cared for the environment. In addition, the book includes portraits of folk heroes from the different cultures that make up our country.

As you read these stories, you can share in the humor that helped lighten the burdens of early American settlers and Native Americans. You will also feel the spirit of courage that lies behind each folk legend.

Mike Fink and a fellow scout spot an Indian on the riverbank.

CHAPTER

HEROES OF OUR NATION'S BIRTH

The Revolutionary War gave birth to a new nation, the United States of America. The thirteen American colonies had originally been ruled by Britain. As a result of the war, they won their independence from Britain. The war started on April 19, 1775, when colonial soldiers battled the British army at Lexington, Massachusetts. After it was over, the separate colonies had to learn how to work together as one nation. The new country experienced many changes. As it developed, it became an example to the rest of the world of a free nation governed by its own people.

The stories that spread during this time told of heroic men and women. Ethan Allen, for example, fought bravely with the Green Mountain Boys, and Molly Pitcher worked tirelessly on the battlefield at Monmouth.

Opposite:
A soldier holding a musket and flag proudly displays "The Spirit of '76."

Ethan Allen: Brave Patriot

It was about 3:00 a.m. on May 10, 1775, just three weeks after the start of the Revolutionary War. A rowdy group of eighty-three settlers stood outside Fort Ticonderoga in the New York colony, preparing to attack the British who were sleeping within the fort. They were the Green Mountain Boys, led by a man named Ethan Allen. Silently they crept through a hole in the fort's wall and surprised the lone guard. The guard aimed his gun at Ethan Allen, but the gun misfired. Allen claimed the fort "in the name of the Great Jehovah and the Continental Congress." The British immediately surrendered. Ethan Allen and the Green Mountain Boys had taken Fort Ticonderoga without firing a shot!

The victory at Fort Ticonderoga made heroes of the Green Mountain Boys. Up to this time, many people in New York considered them troublemakers. Since 1770, they had been fighting a land war, not against the British, but against the "Yorkers."

Ethan Allen and his troops lived west of the Green Mountains in what was known as the New Hampshire Grants (today the state of Vermont). They had bought this land from New Hampshire, but in 1764, the British ruled that the land belonged to New York. Six years later, when New York courts ruled that the land titles in the Grants were not valid, the settlers were ordered to buy their land a second time.

The settlers were angered by this decision. Ethan Allen and Seth Warner, another settler,

Ethan Allen
demands entrance
to Fort
Ticonderoga.

organized the Green Mountain Boys to resist the ruling. The group had no standard muskets and not a single cannon. They had no uniforms, but they all wore a sprig of evergreen in their hats.

When the Revolutionary War began in 1775, the Green Mountain Boys joined the patriots. Their early morning victory at Fort Ticonderoga was one of the first important American victories.

During the war, one of Allen's main causes was for Vermont to become a state. He made several attempts to try and achieve this goal, but he was unsuccessful.

In the fall of 1775, Ethan Allen planned an attack on Montreal, Canada. He was captured and spent three years as a prisoner of war in England. In 1778, he was released and returned to America to become a colonel in the Continental Army.

Ethan Allen retired to a farm in Burlington, Vermont in 1787, and died on February 12, 1789. Two years later, Vermont became the fourteenth state.

Even before his death, heroic stories had begun spreading about Ethan Allen. Some people told how he had ridden a moose down a river as a young boy. Others said that he could bite off nails with his teeth or strangle a bear with his bare hands. They also claimed he stood as tall as a maple tree.

In one tale, Ethan Allen got caught in a blizzard while walking in the woods. His clothes were soon soaked. To keep from freezing to death, he marked out a path in a circle and walked it all night.

These stories showed the admiration the settlers had for Ethan Allen. They knew he had a temper. And he was known for his strong opinions. But to this day, Ethan Allen is honored in Vermont for his bravery.

Molly Pitcher (Mary Hays)

Like many wives of Revolutionary War soldiers, Mary Hays (known as Molly) followed her husband, John, as he and his regiment traveled from battle to battle. Along with other women, Mary did washing and cooking and cared for wounded soldiers. During her travels with the troops, Mary also learned how to fire a cannon.

Although it is fairly certain that Mary Hays was present at the Battle of Monmouth, New Jersey, on June 28, 1778, no one is really sure what she actually did there. The most popular version of the story says that on that scorching summer day, Mary devoted herself to carrying pitchers of cool water from a nearby well to the soldiers who were collapsing as much from the heat as from their wounds. She made trip after trip between the battlefield and the well, filling a pitcher with water to share with the weary soldiers. It was getting hotter and hotter. Mary scurried back and forth, swabbing blood, cleaning and wrapping wounds, and offering water and cool rags to the men. As the story goes, men began to call for her: "Molly! Pitcher, please! Molly, Pitcher!" From that day on, she was known as Molly Pitcher.

There are other stories of Mary at Monmouth that make her seem even more heroic. One tells how, as she made her trips back and forth between the well, Molly often passed by her husband's cannon, checking to see if he was all right. Popular legend has it that on one trip she found him collapsed from the heat beside his cannon. Mary picked up the rammer staff, loaded, and fired. She supposedly continued firing throughout the afternoon, until dark, when the battlefield fell silent.

After the battle—another story says—General George Washington wished to meet the brave woman who had fired the cannon at Monmouth. "Madam, who are you?" Washington reportedly asked. "Mary Hays, sir. They call me Molly." "You are now Sergeant Molly," the general responded.

Although the details about Mary Hays's role at Monmouth vary, and it is not known how much is fact

Molly Pitcher takes her husband's place after he collapses during the battle of Monmouth.

and how much is fiction, her life after the Revolution is fairly well documented. In 1783, Mary and her husband moved to Carlisle, Pennsylvania, where John became a barber. After his death in 1793, Mary remarried. When John McCauly, her second husband, died in 1813, Mary worked mostly as a nurse. In 1822, the state of Pennsylvania awarded her $40 a year for her contributions during the Revolution. Mary Hays died ten years later, on January 26, 1832.

Old Stormalong: Able-bodied Seaman

Alfred Bulltop Stormalong was the gigantic hero of sailors' tall tales and songs. To pass the time on long voyages, sailors made up stories about Old Stormie. Each sailor tried to outdo his shipmates with more fantastic tales.

Some sailors said Stormie was born in a village along the Maine coast. Others said he was born near Cape Cod in Massachusetts. He first went to sea as a cabin boy when he was twelve or thirteen years old. Stormie was so tall that he kept hitting his head on the "overheads," or ships' ceilings.

By the time he was full-grown, Stormie supposedly stood four or five fathoms tall. A fathom is the way sailors measure the sea's depth. One fathom is equal to six feet, so you can see that Stormie was at least twenty-four feet tall. But not all sailors agreed. In some tales, Stormie was as tall as fourteen fathoms. Probably what happened was that he got a little taller each time his stories were retold.

In one story, Stormie saved his ship. The captain had given the order to hoist the anchor. But no matter how hard the sailors pulled, they couldn't budge it. Stormie stuck a knife between his teeth and dived into the sea. After he disappeared, the sea churned. The ship pitched and tossed on the wild waves. Just when it seemed that the ship might sink, Stormie popped to the surface. He climbed on board and yanked up the anchor. Stormie explained that he'd had a little fight with an octopus, who was holding the anchor with

Stormie's ship reels in the violent waves.

FRANCIS MARION: THE SWAMP FOX

"The Spirit of '76" was the phrase used to describe the feeling among American patriots during the Revolutionary War. It was a mighty force. It caused men and women to undertake very brave deeds. And many writers, through pamphlets, stories, ballads, and songs, turned several of America's patriots into unbelievably heroic individuals whose lives seemed more interesting than almost everyone else's.

One such patriot was Francis Marion of South Carolina, an officer of the Revolutionary War. Because of the clever tricks he used to outsmart the British during battles and his ability to move quickly through the woods without being noticed, Marion came to be known as the "Swamp Fox." One popular tale has him signaling to his men by crying out like a swamp fox. Since this animal is not found anywhere in America, that part of the story is a little unlikely.

One legend about Francis Marion that has lasted through the years concerns an attack on the British at Black Mingo River. As the story goes, Marion wanted to surprise the British, who were stationed at the river, and capture their camp. When Marion's horses started galloping across a plank bridge, their hooves could be plainly heard. The British were warned! Marion then ordered an attack on the camp. The capture was successful, but it was said that, during the rest of the war, Marion never again crossed a bridge at night without first having his men put down blankets to muffle the sound of the horses' hooves as they approached.

four tentacles. With the other four, the creature grasped the bottom of the sea. Stormie tied each arm into a different sailor's knot and freed the anchor.

Another story invented by sailors told how Stormie had helped win the Revolutionary War. He supposedly fought with John Paul Jones, the captain of the *Poor Richard.* Jones was battling the *Serapis,* a ship of the British navy. Cannonballs from the *Serapis* made huge holes in the side of the *Poor Richard*. To keep the boat from sinking, Stormie lashed together the masts of the two ships. He led the American sailors as they jumped aboard the *Serapis* and took control of the ship.

Part of the fun of the Stormalong tales was inventing new stories. No ship was ever big enough for Stormie—until he built his own. Most sailors called it the *Courser*. She was so large that it took a sailor on horseback an entire day to ride from stem to stern. The masts were hinged so they would bend when the sun and moon went by. Sailors who climbed to the crow's nest to serve as lookouts went up as young men. When they came down, they had gray beards.

Another time, the *Courser* tried to sail through the English Channel, but there wasn't enough room. Stormie had the crew swab the ship's sides with soap. The ship managed to squeak through, leaving soap all over the cliffs. This supposedly explains why the cliffs of Dover, on England's coast, are white.

Lots of different tales are told about how Old Stormalong died. But most sailors agree that it was the coming of the steamship that did him in. For years after, sailors made up songs about Stormie. And to this day, all seamen first-class put "A.B.S." after their names. Most people think that these initials mean able-bodied seaman, which they do. But Yankee sailors like to say that they stand for the first and best able-bodied seaman—Alfred Bulltop Stormalong.

CHAPTER

2

LEGENDS OF OUR COUNTRY'S GROWTH

The period after the Revolutionary War was a time of great growth in America. In 1775, the frontiersman Daniel Boone opened up the western wilderness to settlement. He blazed a 300-mile trail called the Wilderness Road. Mountain men and fur trappers soon returned with wonderful stories about a rugged land west of the Appalachian Mountains. Explorers such as Lewis and Clark made maps of the land and rivers all the way to the Pacific Coast. Wagon trains of settlers pushed the frontier farther and farther west. The railroad began to make travel easier, but most Americans still lived on farms.

Many tall tales grew up in the late 1700s and early 1800s, when the United States was a young nation. Men who worked on riverboats boasted about the dangers they faced and the critters they had licked.

Opposite: Long wagon trains traveled hundreds of miles, transporting families and their belongings.

They told stories about the most famous riverboat worker, Mike Fink. Gentle Johnny Appleseed left his mark by planting apple orchards throughout the East. Daring frontiersmen such as Davy Crockett explored the wilderness to the west. Railroad workers told tales about John Henry, the man who beat a machine. Slaves facing unimaginable hardships drew strength from stories about High John the Conqueror.

Mike Fink: King of the Keelboat Captains

"I'm a ring-tailed roarer! I'm a regular screamer! WHOOP! I'm half wild horse, half alligator, and half snapping turtle. I can out-run, out-shoot, out-fight, and out-brag any man on either side of the Mississippi!"

Legend has it that Mike Fink could brag like this for thirty minutes or more—and never repeat himself. He was the most famous of all the keelboat captains, as good at fighting and shooting as he was at bragging. So much has been written about him that it's hard to tell what is fact and what is fiction.

Mike Fink was born at old Fort Pitt (now Pittsburgh) in 1770. As a youth, he quickly earned fame as an Indian scout and expert marksman. One story describes how at age sixteen Mike beat several adults in a shooting contest. Each entrant had five chances to hit a bull's-eye. Young Mike Fink hit the bull's-eye on the first try. But his other shots left no marks on the target. Everyone thought he'd missed— until they looked closely at the bull's-eye. All five bullets had passed through the same hole and were lined up in a row.

During the early 1800s, before the steamboat was invented, most shipping was done on keelboats—flat-bottomed boats that could carry more than sixty tons of cargo under their roofed decks. Mike Fink worked on keelboats along the Ohio and Mississippi rivers. He eventually became captain of his own boat, the *Lightfoot.*

The easy part of a keelboat voyage was going downstream. But to go upstream, a great deal of strength was required to pole the heavy boats against the current. On each boat, one man wore a red feather in his cap, meaning that he was the strongest, toughest man on his boat. Mike aimed to get himself a red feather right away—and he did. Many stories are told about how Mike wanted to be the toughest man on both the Ohio and Mississippi rivers.

Mike Fink wins a shooting match with Davy Crockett.

Supposedly, Mike soon had so many red feathers that he threw some of them away, so no one would think he was a bonfire.

According to legend, Mike Fink beat Davy Crockett in a shooting match. They drove nails into trees, put out candles, and shot flies off a cow's horn. Both did equally

Keelboats curved
upward on the
ends, and had a
cabin in the center.
Keelboats could be
powered by a sail
when there was
enough wind.

well—until Mike Fink shot half of a comb from his wife's head without moving a hair. Davy gave the victory to Mike and said his hand would shake too much if he tried to shoot at a lady.

No man, animal, or machine could outdo the mighty Mike Fink—until the coming of the steamboat. These paddle wheelers took over all of the river trade. They could carry passengers and cargo faster than any keelboat. According to legend, Mike refused to give way to any man or boat. He ran his keelboat into the side of the steamboat, and both boats sank.

Whether or not this story is true, Mike left the river and began to work as a boatman and a trapper. In 1823, he was killed on his first expedition. Stories differ about how Mike died. But nearly all tales agree that he was killed in a shooting match. Most likely, it was the result of a quarrel. Whatever the cause, many creative tales describe Mike Fink's last words. The stories say he whispered, "I was king of the keelboatmen."

Johnny Appleseed: Pioneer Planter

On September 26, 1774, a baby boy was born in Leominster, Massachusetts. His name was John Chapman. He would come to be known as Johnny Appleseed. Johnny was a pioneer who spent his life planting apple trees on the frontier during the 1800s.

People invented colorful stories about Johnny Appleseed's deeds, but few details are known about his early life. His mother and baby brother died before he was two. His father remarried. Some historians believe that Johnny lived with his father, stepmother, and their ten children.

That's about all that's known of Johnny's life until he was twenty-three. The year was 1797. Johnny began to plant apple trees all over the western frontier, traveling alone from western Pennsylvania through Ohio, Illinois, and Indiana. During the War of 1812, Johnny served as a frontier messenger. He would run many miles to warn Ohio settlers of the danger of an Indian attack.

The tales that were created about Johnny told of how he walked the wilderness barefooted, with a sugar sack for a shirt and his cooking pot for a hat. Other stories described how Johnny slept outdoors. While most men carried guns, Johnny carried a pouch of apple seeds.

Settlers also told of Johnny's religious beliefs. Many said he was never without his Bible and a bundle of religious pamphlets. He liked to talk about what he read in the Bible.

Johnny Appleseed.

Supposedly, Johnny was extremely careful never to hurt animals. In one story, he put out his campfire because it was killing mosquitoes. Some people claimed that he talked to birds. When Johnny found a wolf in a trap, he supposedly freed the wounded animal and nursed it back to health. After that, the wolf went everywhere with Johnny, according to some settlers.

Johnny died in a settler's cabin in Fort Wayne, Indiana, on March 10, 1845. No one knows for sure exactly where he is buried, but a gravestone was put up to honor him. On it are the words, "He lived for others."

After Johnny's death, the tales about him got bigger and bigger. Some people said he planted trees all the way to the Pacific Coast. Others said his ghost would come to help anyone who was lost in the forest. These imaginative details helped make Johnny Appleseed a folk legend.

Davy Crockett: A Frontier Superman

Davy Crockett was a frontiersman who was born on August 17, 1786, in Greene County, Tennessee. At various times, he was a scout, soldier, and member of the U.S. Congress. His motto was "Be sure you're right—then go ahead!" Many exaggerated stories were told about Davy's fantastic feats—some of these tales were told or written by Davy himself.

According to many of the tales, Davy learned to shoot before he learned to walk or talk. He could outrun a deer, stare down a bear, and grin a raccoon right out of a tree. He had a pet bear named Death Hug and a pet alligator named Old Mississippi.

Davy Crockett.

When Davy was in Congress, so the story goes, a comet was expected to hit the earth. To prevent this from happening, Davy climbed to the top of the Appalachian Mountains, grabbed the speeding comet by the tail, whirled it around, and sent it flying back out into space.

The real Davy Crockett came from a poor family. He worked to help pay the family's debts. When he was twenty, he married Polly Finley. They had three children. When Polly died several years later, Davy married Elizabeth Patton, a young widow with two children. The Crocketts moved several times, each time farther west into the Tennessee wilderness. He tried farming, but he was happier hunting. From 1813 to 1814, Davy worked as a scout for Andrew Jackson and later earned the rank of colonel in the Tennessee militia.

In 1817, Davy began his political career. He served as a justice of the peace for Lawrence County, Tennessee. His homespun style and humorous campaign speeches earned him election to the Tennessee legislature in 1821 and in 1823. He was also elected to serve three times in the U.S. House of Representatives. During one of his campaigns, Davy claimed that the local animals wanted him elected. When his opponent was speaking, a flock of hens clucked "Cr-cr-kt" so loudly that no one could hear him. Davy claimed the hens were saying "Crockett."

After serving in Congress, Davy Crockett fought in the battle of the Alamo in San Antonio. English-speaking Texans had decided to break away from Mexico to form their own republic. Davy Crockett, James Bowie, and William Travis led the 184 Texans in a losing battle against about 6,000 Mexicans. While defending the Alamo, all of them were killed. Davy Crockett died at the Alamo on March 6, 1836. But his courage in battle added to his larger-than-life image.

After his death, stories about Davy—both written and those passed on by word of mouth—began to grow. Between 1835 and 1856, a series of small paperback books was published. They were known as the *Davy Crockett Almanacks* and contained tales of highly exaggerated deeds. No one knows for certain who wrote them. Since that time, Davy has been the subject of other books as well as songs, movies, and television programs. Along with Davy's own writings, they helped build the legend of this frontier hero.

HIGH JOHN THE CONQUERER

To slaveholders, slaves were something to be owned, like a horse or a pair of shoes. But slaveholders could never own the soul of a slave, or stop slaves from thinking and dreaming of freedom. To face their hardships, slaves made up stories.

One group of stories developed about High John the Conqueror. He was a clever slave who did as little slave labor as possible. In some tales, High John would start to use a hoe, and it would mysteriously break. Or he'd begin to plow the field, and his mule team would "accidentally" trample the crops. Here is one of the many tales in which High John used his wits to outsmart—and conquer—his master.

One day, Old Master announced that slaves could catch any fish in his pond—except catfish. The slaves had to throw the catfish back. The only fish left to keep were perch, which were so tiny that they were almost all bones.

High John decided he'd fish for catfish, despite what the Old Master had said. One day, after catching a bucketful of perch, he hung a huge catfish from a tree. Who should come along then but Old Master! High John had to think fast to get out of this scrape.

Old Master asked, "How's the fishing, High John?" High John answered, "At first I caught a mess of perch. But then that catfish hanging there began to steal my bait. I asked him to stop, but he wouldn't. So I had no choice but to catch him. Since I'm done fishing now, I may as well throw him back."

Before Old Master had a chance to reply, High John tossed the catfish back into the pond. He picked up his pole and bucket and strolled away. Old Master just shook his head as he watched the ripples on the pond grow wider.

John Henry: Amazing Steel Driver

For African-American railroad workers in the 1880s, John Henry was their hero. He was a steel driver who worked on the Big Bend Tunnel for the Chesapeake and Ohio Railroad. The tunnel had to go through a mountain. To build it, workers drove steel rods into the rock with their hammers. They put explosives into the holes made by the rods and blew up the rock. One worker, the "shaker," held the spike. His partner, the "driver," stood back and pounded at the steel with a ten-pound hammer.

There really was such a tunnel and there really was such a man as John Henry. But beyond that, the details of his life have become exaggerated. He became famous in a folk ballad and many stories.

According to legend, a man brought a new machine to the tunnel one day. It was a steam drill. John Henry and his foreman bet that John Henry could beat the steam drill in a race. John Henry was so

John Henry and his fellow railroad builders work tirelessly to build a railroad tunnel through a mountain.

THE BALLAD OF JOHN HENRY

The legend of John Henry was so popular that more than fifty versions of the John Henry ballad exist today. Here is the first verse of one of these ballads set to music.

The remaining eleven verses tell of how John Henry "broke his poor heart" and died trying to "whop that steel on down" into the rock with his hammer to beat out the man with the steam drill.

John Henry

Traditional

When John Hen-ry was a lit-tle ba - by,—
Set - tin' on his mam-my's knee,— Said,
"Big Bend — Tun-nel on the C. and O. — 'Road,
Gon-na be the death – of — me, Lord, – Lord,
Gon-na be the death – of — me." Said, me."

big that he used a twenty-pound hammer. He hit the rods so fast that they smoked. Some people said he even swung two hammers at a time. In thirty-five minutes, John Henry supposedly drilled two seven-foot holes. The steam drill bored only one hole that was nine feet deep.

John Henry won the bet, but he died that day. The stories and songs tell different tales about his death. Some say that he lay down and died because he was so tired. Others say that he died of a burst blood vessel. But most of the legends agree that he died, as he lived, with a hammer in his hand.

In all the songs and stories, John Henry became a giant of a man. He probably wasn't eight feet tall. But he had a giant spirit. He has come to stand for the battle of the worker against the machine. John Henry represents the desire to try hard and do well.

C H A P T E R

FOLK HEROES OF THE WILD WEST

Between 1861 and 1865, America's energies were taken up by the Civil War. As the North fought against the South in this bloody battle, little attention could be devoted to anything else. When the war ended, however, many who had fought in it traveled west in search of new opportunities on the frontier. Thousands of others followed, drawn by stories of free land and discoveries of gold. Overnight, towns such as Deadwood City, South Dakota, sprung up. Many of these towns had more saloons than homes or churches. Ranchers established huge ranges for grazing cattle, and cowboys came to run the cattle drives. Railroad builders laid down tracks to ship the cattle and transport passengers. They hired men such as William "Buffalo Bill" Cody to kill the buffalo that got in the way of the trains. Telegraph companies

Opposite: Although an outlaw, Jesse James was so admired by the public that "The Jesse James Stories" were published about him in a weekly magazine. This scene is from the cover of the first issue.

strung lines along the tracks. Change was coming to the West, especially for the American Indians of the Great Plains.

The heroes of this period reflect the rough nature of the West. There were outlaws, such as the bank and train robber Jesse James. Women of the period, like Calamity Jane, were independent and often relied on their own wits instead of on men. Cowboys such as Deadwood Dick helped build a romantic picture of life on the range. But none of their deeds were as wild as those of Pecos Bill, the mythical westerner who supposedly invented cowpunching.

Jesse James: Robin Hood or Merciless Killer?

Was Jesse James an evil man or a Robin Hood, who took from the rich and gave to the poor? This question is part of what made Jesse James a folk legend.

There is no doubt that Jesse James robbed and murdered. He led about twenty-five robberies in Missouri and other states and killed at least sixteen men. Jesse's life of crime had its start during the Civil War. He joined his brother Frank in a gang led by men who sided with the Confederacy. After the war, the James brothers formed a new gang with the Younger brothers. In 1866, the gang robbed the First National Bank in Liberty, Missouri. This was the first daylight bank robbery to take place in the United States in peacetime, and it attracted a great deal of attention. The James-Younger band committed their first train robbery in 1873. Three years later, three gang members were killed, and three were captured as they tried to rob a Minnesota bank. Only Jesse and Frank were able to escape.

They both went into hiding. Jesse moved to St. Joseph, Missouri, with his family. He went by the name Thomas Howard and posed as a cattle buyer.

By then, there was a $10,000 price on Jesse's head. The reward made Jesse a tempting target, even to those people he thought were on his side. One night, two former gang members showed up at Jesse's house. Charles and Robert Ford were going to plan another robbery with

Jesse James (seated left), Frank James (seated right), Cole Younger (standing left), and Bob Younger (standing right).

Jesse. But the robbery never took place. On April 13, 1882, Robert Ford shot Jesse James in the back of the head while Jesse was straightening a picture on the wall. Ford then claimed the reward.

Jesse James became a hero. A folk ballad was written about him. It called Robert Ford "a dirty little coward" and described Jesse as "a friend of the poor."

Stories were made up to show the "good side" of Jesse James. After robbing a bank, he and his gang

Jesse James.

supposedly burst into a farmhouse at gunpoint. They found a sobbing young widow who told them she owed the bank $1,200. She would lose her farm if she didn't pay that day. From the money he had just stolen, Jesse gave her what she needed. He also gave her another $300 to buy shoes for her children and repair her barn. Then the gang hid and waited for the bank official to collect the money from the widow. They robbed him and got back their money—minus the $300 they had given the widow.

What does history say about Jesse James? There is no proof that he ever gave money to the poor. And, even though Jesse said he killed only in self-defense, records show, for example, that during a train robbery on July 15, 1881, he shot the conductor and a passenger in cold blood. Legends about Jesse also claim that he taught a church choir. But his family reported that he couldn't even carry a tune.

Why, then, did Jesse become a folk hero? Many farmers at the time had no quarrel with him or his gang. It seemed romantic that the gang robbed only banks, railroads, and express companies that had a lot of money. As more and more stories were told about Jesse and more people sang his ballad, Jesse's evil actions were ignored.

Calamity Jane (Martha Jane Cannary)

Mystery surrounds the life of Calamity Jane, and the details that are available vary from one story to another. Was she a Pony Express rider? Did she serve with General George Armstrong Custer? Did she really marry Wild Bill Hickok?

Most historians believe that she was born in Princeton, Missouri, on May 1, 1852. She was the oldest of five children. Jane spent lots of time outdoors and learned to ride at an early age. In 1865, her family left for Utah. Her mother died on the way, and her father died soon after they reached Salt Lake City. The other children were placed with foster families, but there are different accounts of what happened to Jane. Some say that she grew up in a series of army posts and mining camps in Montana, Wyoming, and Utah. Others say that she ran away with a young army lieutenant and had a child.

Calamity Jane poses with her rifle.

Those who study the West agree that Jane was rough and rowdy. She became a fearless rider and a crack shot. Jane usually dressed in men's clothing because this suited her rough style of life. She was known to swear, drink too much, and spit tobacco juice. None of this was typical behavior for a woman in those days.

Calamity Jane at Wild Bill Hickok's grave.

Calamity Jane joined gold seekers who moved to Deadwood City, South Dakota, during the gold rush of 1876. According to a woman who lived there at the time, Calamity was a colorful character. She was an interesting mix of bold behavior and kind actions. When smallpox struck Deadwood City in 1878, she cared for the sick. In those days, most people died of smallpox, but Jane was determined to help during the crisis, and she was not worried about catching smallpox herself.

In 1891, she married a man named Clinton Burke, and they had a daughter. After Burke left her, according to Jane, she met Wild Bill Hickok when they both served as scouts for General Custer. She claimed she married Wild Bill in a secret ceremony. There is no evidence, however, that they ever married or that they were even sweethearts.

Calamity Jane returned to Deadwood City when her daughter was seven. Calamity Jane died on August 1, 1903, and was buried next to the grave of Wild Bill Hickok. The townsfolk helped raise money to send Jane's daughter to private school.

There are different stories about how Calamity Jane got her nickname. Some say it came from her wild behavior. Whenever she entered a saloon, legend says that she fired her pistols, shattering the mirrors. People inside would shout, "Here's Calamity!" Another story said she got the name after rescuing her commander during an Indian raid. But Jane said Wild Bill Hickok gave her the nickname.

In 1941, more mystery developed about Calamity Jane. A woman named Jane Hickok McCormick claimed to be Calamity's daughter, Janey. She said she was raised by the O'Neils, wealthy friends of Calamity Jane. When Captain O'Neil was dying, he gave Janey a rawhide box. Inside were a wedding ring and diaries in the form of letters to Janey. Many historians believe the letters are actually from Calamity Jane. Was everything in them true? Probably not. Even so, they add to the legend of Calamity Jane.

Deadwood Dick (Nat Love)

More than 38,000 cowboys drove cattle during the days of the Old West. A quarter of them were African Americans. One cowboy who made a legend of himself was Nat Love, who later claimed the title "Deadwood Dick."

Nat Love was born on a slave plantation in Davidson County, Tennessee. After the Civil War ended, he left home at age fifteen, traveled west, and went to work on a ranch near Dodge City, Kansas. As Nat told it, one of his first jobs was to break in Good Eye, the meanest and toughest horse in the corral.

Much of what we know about Nat Love comes from his autobiography, *The Adventures of Nat Love, Better Known in the Cattle Country as "Deadwood Dick,"* written in 1907. He was the only African-American cowboy to write a full-length book on his

PECOS BILL: LEGENDARY COWBOY

Pecos Bill, unlike Jesse James, Calamity Jane, and Deadwood Dick, was not a real person. Stories about Pecos Bill were probably first told in the 1870s, but it wasn't until 1923 that they appeared in writing in an article in *Century* magazine. Soon, many other stories were being written about this man who supposedly taught broncos how to buck and invented cowpunching, branding, the six-shooter, and the lariat.

According to these stories, Bill was born in Texas. When he was a baby, his family decided to move west where it was less crowded. Bill's parents loaded their seventeen children into the covered wagon and set off toward the sunset. Somewhere along the way, Bill fell out. He was rescued by coyotes, who raised him.

With each new story, more exciting adventures were invented about Bill. He caught a mountain lion, which he rode like a saddle horse. He used a giant snake wrapped around his arm as a lariat. On a bet, he saddled a cyclone and rode it from Oklahoma across three states. The cyclone couldn't buck him off, so in desperation it "rained out" from under him. Bill landed in California, where he supposedly created Death Valley with the force of his fall.

Most storytellers say that Bill met his true love, Slue-Foot Sue, after he saw her riding down the Rio Grande on a huge catfish. On their wedding day, Sue insisted that she ride Bill's horse, Widow-Maker. For three days and four nights, she bounced higher and higher until she landed on the moon. Bill began to howl, and the coyotes soon copied him, which is why, to this day, coyotes howl at the moon.

experiences in the Wild West. There is probably some truth in what he wrote, but most historians believe that he exaggerated wildly. For example, Nat wrote that he had been shot fourteen times, but had no scars. He also claimed that he once rode his horse into a saloon and ordered two drinks—one for himself and one for his horse. And he wrote about how, when he got into trouble trying to rope and steal a U.S. Army cannon, a lawman named Bat Masterson came to his rescue. In addition, he told of being adopted by an American Indian tribe after being captured in battle. He then escaped, so said Nat, by riding bareback twelve hours across the prairie.

Nat earned the nickname "Deadwood Dick" after winning the roping and shooting contests at a Deadwood City rodeo. He hit the bull's-eye with all fourteen shots from his rifle. He also hit the target with ten out of ten shots from his Colt .45 pistol. Nat Love was the first, but not the only, one to use this name. The original name was created by Edward L. Wheeler. He was a writer of novels, whose hero, "Deadwood Dick," had adventures on the open range.

The coming of the railroad spelled the end of the cowboy era because cattle could be more cheaply shipped by rail. In 1890, Nat Love took a job as a Pullman porter. This was one of the few jobs then open to African Americans. Nat wrote that he didn't object to the job, and he did appreciate tips. In his life on the rails, Deadwood Dick traveled across many of the same areas he had roamed on horseback.

Nat Love with his lariat and saddle.

CHAPTER 4

LEGENDS IN LITERATURE

The stories of folk heroes, real or imagined, were originally passed on by word of mouth. Tales were told around the campfire or in the cramped quarters of sailing ships. They helped people pass the time on long journeys by covered wagon or riverboat. Eventually, the stories came to be written down so that there would be a permanent record of them.

In addition to literature about people who actually existed, there were tales about characters invented by writers. One such character who had absolutely no basis in history was the lumberjack Paul Bunyan. Another character, Hiawatha, was made famous in a poem by Henry Wadsworth Longfellow. Many stories about Iktomi, a Sioux Indian trickster, have also been written down and illustrated with Native American artwork.

Opposite:
Hiawatha was a great peacemaker who helped to create the Iroquois League of Five Nations. This illustration is from an 1897 edition of Longfellow's *The Song of Hiawatha*.

41

Hiawatha: Indian Leader and Hero

Hiawatha is one of the best-known American Indians. Many parks, forests, and roads throughout the country are named after him. But not many people know that there are two Hiawathas and therefore two sets of Hiawatha stories. One story tells the beautiful tale of a make-believe hero. The other is based on a real Native American who is thought to have lived during the mid-1500s.

Most people know about Hiawatha from the 1855 book-length poem, *The Song of Hiawatha.* Its author, Henry Wadsworth Longfellow, used many European ideas about Native American culture and customs to paint a romantic picture of Indian life.

Longfellow's Hiawatha was a young chief who performed amazing deeds, such as outrunning arrows shot through the air. A leader, he tried to prepare his people for the coming of settlers and Christianity. The poem also portrays his grief at the death of his wife, the princess Minnehaha. It ends with Hiawatha paddling his canoe toward the setting sun.

Hiawatha mourning the death of Minnehaha as illustrated in Longfellow's poem.

The life of the real Hiawatha was, in many ways, more amazing. An Iroquois leader, he is thought of as one of the world's most important peacemakers. He helped develop the League of Five Nations, which was a union of tribes that many historians believe influenced the American leaders who later developed our constitutional form of government.

42

At the time when Hiawatha lived, the Iroquois tribes continually raided one another's villages. They burned down homes, killing many.

Most of what we know about Hiawatha and his people comes from stories passed down by Iroquois elders. They tell about one evil tribe member named Atotarho. Legends about him describe how he ate people. The storytellers say that Atotarho murdered Hiawatha's wife and daughters. According to tribal customs, Hiawatha was expected to kill Atotarho in revenge. But Hiawatha was tired of all the killing. He went out into the woods and built a lodge, where he lived all by himself.

It is said that one day, a man from another tribe stopped by Hiawatha's lodge. His name was Deganawidah. He was well known as the Peacemaker because he wanted the Iroquois tribes to finally stop fighting and join together in peace. Hiawatha and the Peacemaker made a plan in which the five tribes would unite to form a central government. Each tribe would be represented. All revenge killings were to stop. Instead, the murderer would pay the victim's family.

Hiawatha and the Peacemaker created a set of laws. According to the laws, federation tribes had to meet every few years, especially if a tribe needed to discuss a problem. They recorded important events on beaded belts, some of which can now be seen in museums. The League of Five Nations lasted about three hundred years, until the Revolutionary War.

IKTOMI: SIOUX TRICKSTER

Iktomi is the hero of many Native American stories. He is a trickster who tries to get the better of others, but usually ends up getting tricked himself instead. All Native American tribes have stories about such a trickster. He is known by a variety of names, including Coyote, Manabozo, Wihio, and Veho. There is no one correct version of these stories. Each storyteller uses familiar themes and develops variations around them. Often the stories teach a moral, or lesson, or explain part of nature.

One such story is about Iktomi and the boulder. Iktomi was walking in his best clothes. But he soon became so hot that he was sorry he had brought his blanket.

"Grandfather Boulder," Iktomi said, "I will give you my blanket to keep the sun off you."

Iktomi spread the blanket on the rock and walked away. But when it began to rain, Iktomi wanted his blanket. He walked back and grabbed it off the boulder.

The rain loosened the boulder, so it crashed down on Iktomi. Iktomi asked the buffalo, elk, antelope, bears, and prairie dogs to roll away the boulder, but they couldn't. Then he told the bats that the boulder had made fun of them. The bats were so angry that they hit the boulder head-on and broke it into pieces. This story was made up to explain why bats have flattened faces and why there are rocks all over the Great Plains.

Paul Bunyan: Giant Lumberjack

Paul Bunyan is the legendary giant lumberjack, the greatest of all loggers, created by someone's wild imagination. No one knows for sure when or where the Paul Bunyan stories got started. A popular belief is that loggers told these tales around the campfire. With each retelling, the stories grew more fantastic.

Paul, as the stories go, weighed fifty pounds within an hour of his birth. He waited until he learned to walk before deciding to be a logger. His first camp was so big that his loggers had to have maps to find their way around. The camp cook flipped hotcakes on a griddle as big as an ice-skating rink. He greased it by having a dozen loggers skate around on it with bacon strapped to their skates.

Many of the Paul Bunyan stories feature Babe, the blue ox. Babe was so huge that he could haul a whole forest of logs. Paul put the camp buildings on wheels so that Babe could move them. When Babe needed new shoes, Paul's blacksmith had to open a new iron mine.

Paul Bunyan carrying a tree on his shoulder.

Supposedly, Paul was responsible for many of America's physical features. He scooped out the Great Lakes to supply drinking water for Babe. He dug Puget Sound in Washington State to float logs to the mill. And after Paul cut down most of the trees on the Great Plains, he made the Rocky Mountains for a windbreak.

A number of these Paul Bunyan tales are old yarns in new settings. Many historians believe that Paul Bunyan served as a model for other folk heroes, such as Pecos Bill.

For Further Reading

Clyne, Patricia Edwards. *Patriots in Petticoats.* New York: Dodd, Mead & Company, 1976.

Goble, Paul. *Iktomi and the Boulder.* New York: Orchard Books, 1988.

Kellogg, Steven. *Johnny Appleseed.* New York: Morrow Junior Books, 1988.

Lisker, Tom. *Tall Tales, American Myths.* Madison, NJ: Raintree Steck-Vaughn, 1977.

Lyman, Nanci A. *Paul Bunyan.* Mahwah, NJ: Troll Associates, 1980.

Miller, Robert. *Reflections of a Black Cowboy: Book 1, Cowboys.* Englewood Cliffs, NJ: Silver Burdett Press, 1991.

Osborne, Mary Pope. *American Tall Tales.* New York: Alfred A. Knopf, 1991.

Sanders, Scott R. *Hear the Wind Blow: American Folk Songs Retold.* New York: Bradbury Press, 1985.

Sanfield, Steve. *The Adventures of High John the Conquerer.* New York: Orchard Books, 1989.

San Souci, Robert D. *Larger Than Life: The Adventures of American Legendary Heroes.* New York: A Doubleday Book for Young Readers, 1991.

Index